STICKER MOSAICS

EASTER

APPLESAUCE PRESS

KENNEBUNKPORT, MAINE

13-Digit ISBN: 978-1-64643-376-6
10-Digit ISBN: 1-64643-376-9

This book may be ordered by mail from the publisher. Please include $5.99 for postage and handling. Please support your local bookseller first!

Books published by Cider Mill Press Book Publishers are available at special discounts for bulk purchases in the United States by corporations, institutions, and other organizations. For more information, please contact the publisher.

Applesauce Press is an imprint of
Cider Mill Press Book Publishers
"Where good books are ready for press"
PO Box 454
12 Spring Street
Kennebunkport, Maine 04046

Visit us online! cidermillpress.com

Typography: Josefin Sans, Industry Inc

Printed in China

1 2 3 4 5 6 7 8 9 0
First Edition

HOW TO USE THIS BOOK

CREATING YOUR OWN STICKER MOSAIC IS SIMPLE. Peel a sticker from the corresponding sticker sheet in the back of the book. You can tear the art pages or sticker sheets out of the book so you don't have to flip back and forth. You will see that each sticker has a number. All you have to do is match the number on the sticker to the number on the silhouette. Once placed, the stickers aren't removable, so put them down carefully. Watch as your Easter puzzles come to life in full color, sticker by sticker!

CONTENTS

7. Fluffy Chick

8. Spring Blossoms

9. Bunny Kisses

10. Garden Chick

11. Festive Pup

12. White Rabbit in the Flowers

Easter Bunny

Spring Lamb

Geese in the Meadow

Three Little Ducklings

Easter Buddies

Little Bluebirds on a Branch

Fluffy Chick

Spring Blossoms

Bunny Kisses

Garden Chick

Festive Pup

White Rabbit in the Flowers

STICKERS

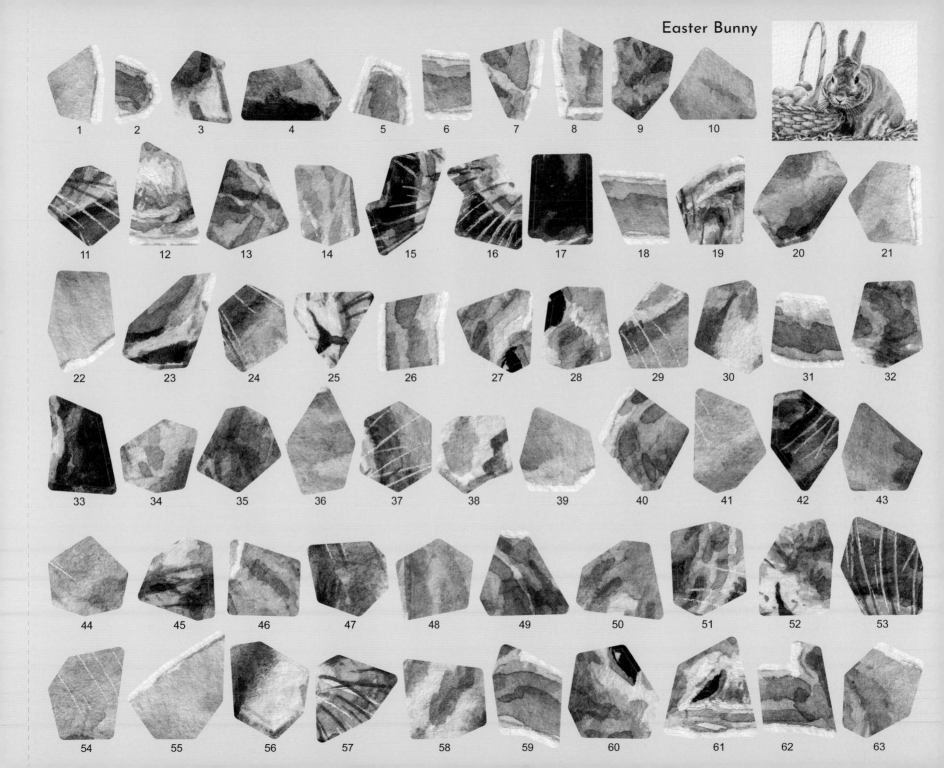

Easter Bunny

Spring Lamb

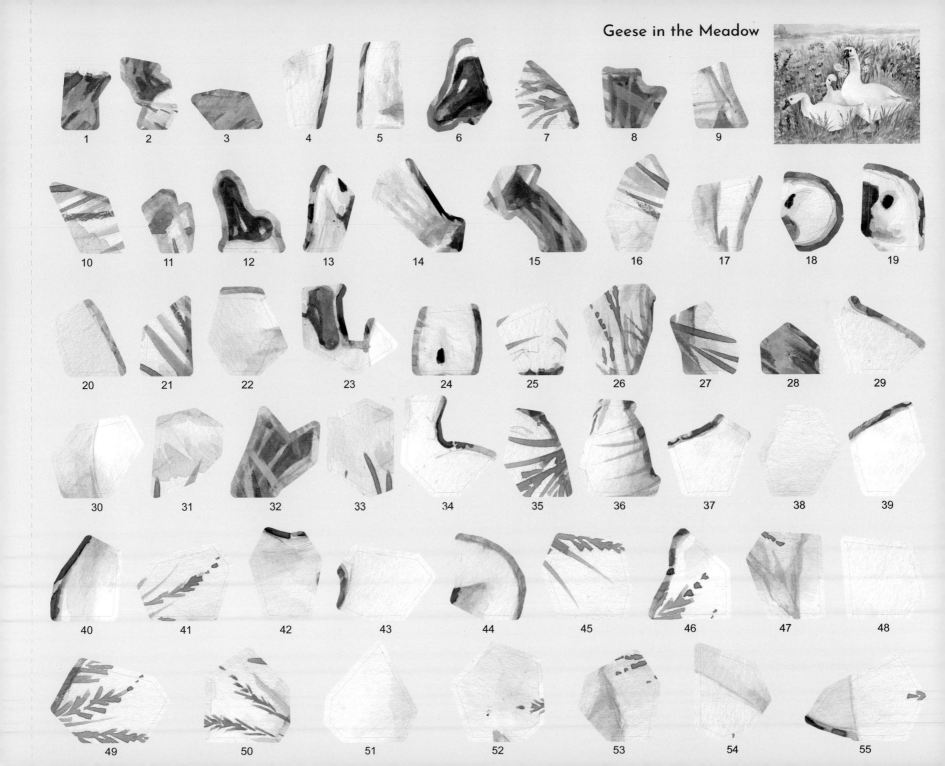

Geese in the Meadow

1 2 3 4 5 6 7 8 9

10 11 12 13 14 15 16 17 18 19

20 21 22 23 24 25 26 27 28 29

30 31 32 33 34 35 36 37 38 39

40 41 42 43 44 45 46 47 48

49 50 51 52 53 54 55

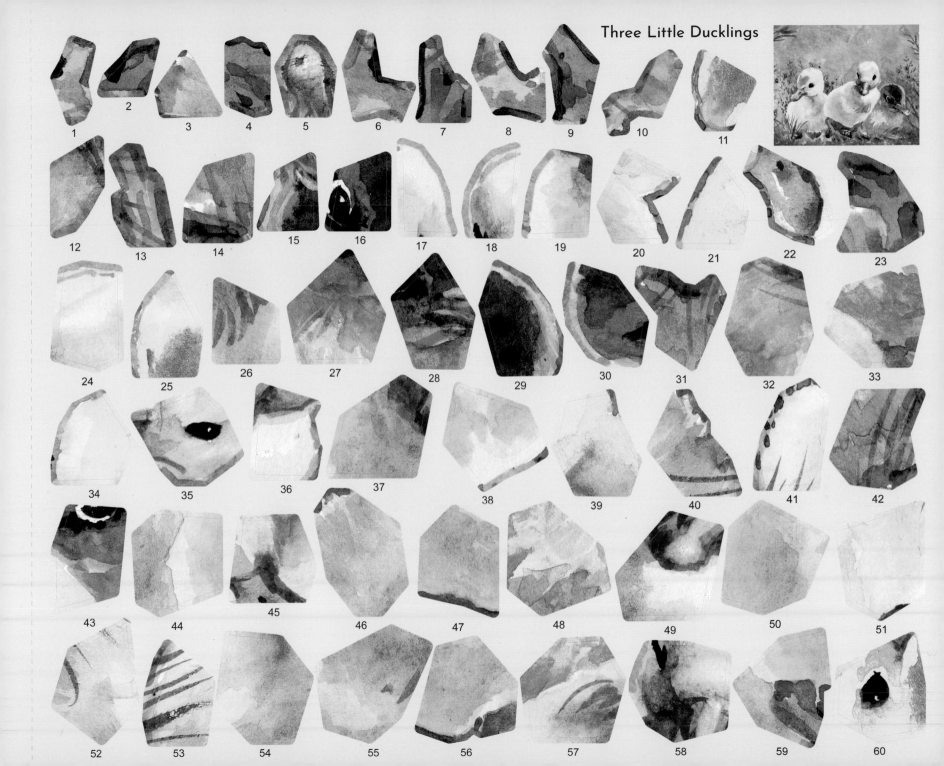

Three Little Ducklings

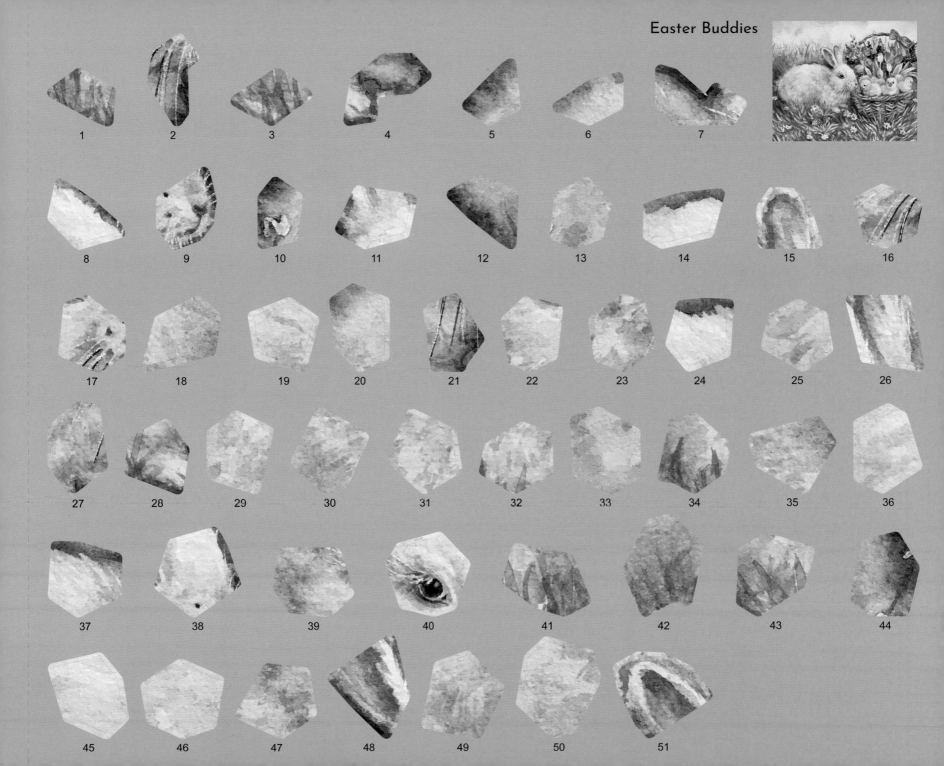

Easter Buddies

1 2 3 4 5 6 7

8 9 10 11 12 13 14 15 16

17 18 19 20 21 22 23 24 25 26

27 28 29 30 31 32 33 34 35 36

37 38 39 40 41 42 43 44

45 46 47 48 49 50 51

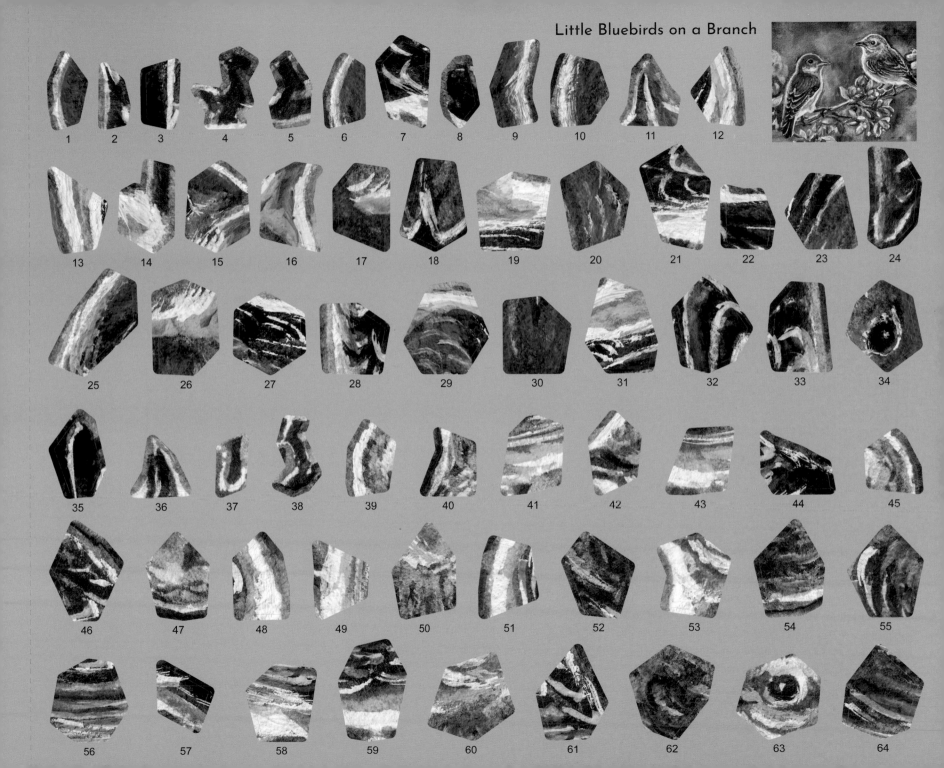

Little Bluebirds on a Branch

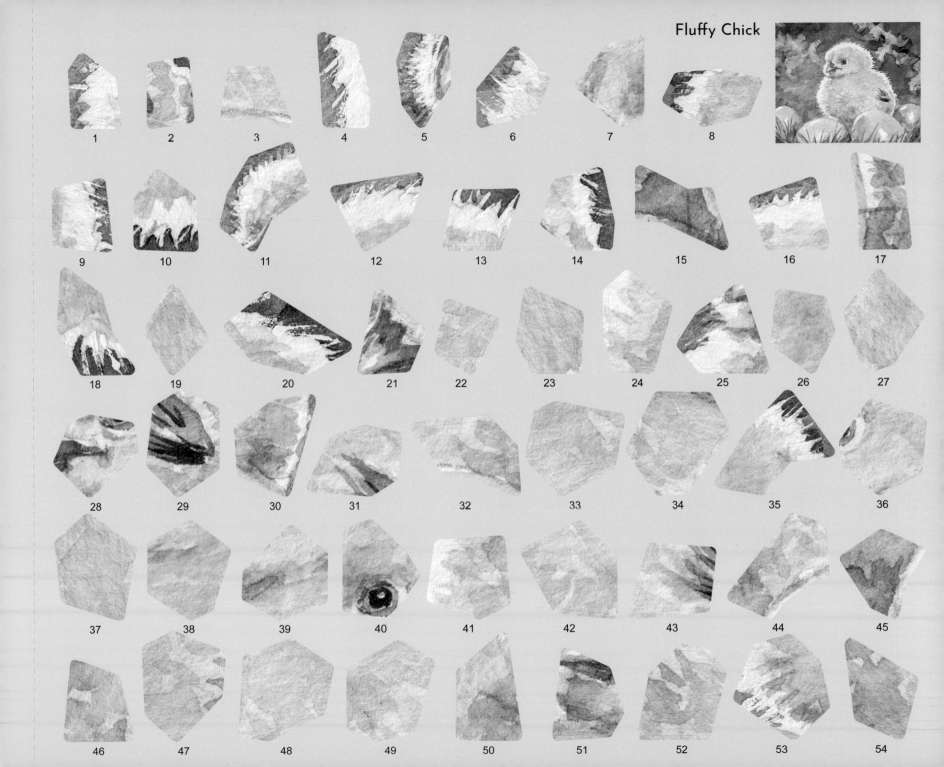

Fluffy Chick

1 2 3 4 5 6 7 8

9 10 11 12 13 14 15 16 17

18 19 20 21 22 23 24 25 26 27

28 29 30 31 32 33 34 35 36

37 38 39 40 41 42 43 44 45

46 47 48 49 50 51 52 53 54

Spring Blossoms

Bunny Kisses

1 2 3 4 5 6 7 8 9 10 11 12 13 14 15 16 17 18 19 20 21 22 23 24 25 26 27 28 29 30 31 32 33 34 35 36 37 38 39 40 41 42 43 44 45 46 47 48 49 50 51 52 53 54 55 56 57 58 59 60 61 62 63 64 65 66 67 68 69 70 71

Garden Chick

1   2   3   4   5   6   7   8

9   10   11   12   13   14   15   16   17

18   19   20   21   22   23   24   25   26   27

28   29   30   31   32   33   34   35   36   37

38   39   40   41   42   43   44   45   46

47   48   49   50   51   52   53   54   55

Festive Pup

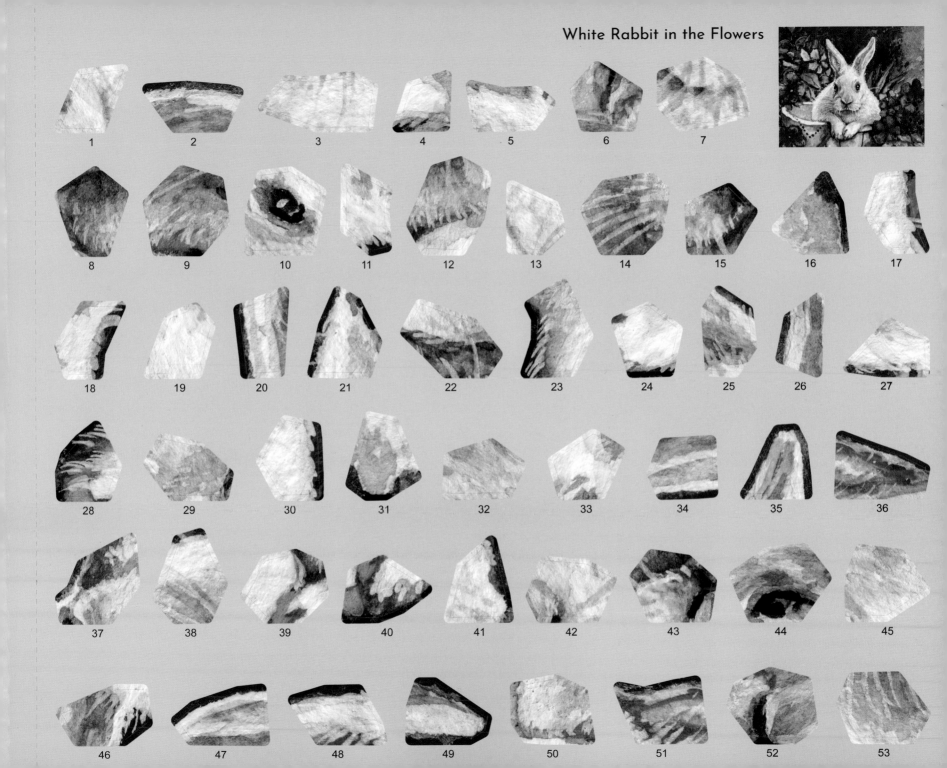

White Rabbit in the Flowers

ABOUT APPLESAUCE PRESS

Good ideas ripen with time. From seed to harvest, Applesauce Press crafts books with beautiful designs, creative formats, and kid-friendly information on a variety of fascinating topics. Like our parent company, Cider Mill Press Book Publishers, our press bears fruit twice a year, publishing a new crop of titles each spring and fall.

Write to us at
PO Box 454
12 Spring Street
Kennebunkport, ME 04046

Or visit us online at
cidermillpress.com